Lady Day

at Emerson's Bar & Grill

by Lanie Robertson

SAMUEL FRENCH, INC.

45 WEST 25TH STREET   **NEW YORK 10010**

7623 SUNSET BOULEVARD   **HOLLYWOOD 90046**

LONDON   *TORONTO*

IMPORTANT BILLING AND CREDIT REQUIREMENTS

All producers of LADY DAY AT EMERSON'S BAR & GRILL *must* give credit to Lanie Robertson in all programs, advertising, publicizing or otherwise exploiting the Play and/or production. Lanie Robertson's name *must* appear on a separate line in which no other name appears, in a size of type not less than 50% the size of type of the title or stars, whichever is the larger. No other name shall preceed the title except the name of any star (there shall be no more than two) and the name of the producer of stock or amateur production.

Billing *must* appear in the following form:

(Name of Producer)
presents

LADY DAY AT EMERSON'S BAR & GRILL

by Lanie Robertson

The following language must also appear on the title page of all theatre programs: "LADY DAY AT EMERSON'S BAR & GRILL was first produced in New York by the Vineyard Theatre."

IN ADDITION: the following credit *must* appear immediately beneath the author's credit whenever and wherever author receives credit, in size of type 33% of the size of title type:

Musical Arrangements by
DANNY HOLGATE

(Note: If special arrangements by Danny Holgate are not used in production, this credit may be deleted.)

LADY DAY AT EMERSON'S BAR & GRILL was first produced at the Alliance Theatre in Atlanta, on April 16, 1986. It was directed by Woodie King, Jr.; musical direction by Neal Tate; setting by Stephen Reardon; lighting design by David Brewer; costumes by Joyce Andrulot; the production manager was Billings LaPierre; the stage manager was John Kirman; assistant director was Karen Robinson; casting director was Jay Binder. The cast was as follows:

Billie Holiday. . . . . Reenie Upchurch
Jimmy Powers. . . . . Neal Tate
Bass Player. . . . . George Grier

LADY DAY AT EMERSON'S BAR & GRILL was produced in New York City at the Vineyard Theatre, on June 5, 1986. It was directed by Andre Ernotte; musical direction by Danny Holgate; set design by William Barclay; lighting design by Phil Monat; costume design by Muriel Stockdale; sound design by Phil Lee; production stage manager was Crystal Huntington; production coordinator. Susan Wilder. The cast was as follows:

Billie Holiday. . . . . Lonette McKee
Jimmy Powers. . . . . Danny Holgate
Guitar Player. . . . . Rudy Stevenson
Bass Player. . . . . David Jackson

This production opened at the Westside Arts Theatre in New York City on Sept. 3, 1986. The role of Billie Holiday in this production was later played by S. Epatha Merkerson.

PLACE:
The action of the play transpires in a small bar in south Philadelphia. Although the bar is presently closed and abandoned, the building still stands on the corner of Fiftieth & Bainbridge Streets. Billie Holiday appeared here in the 1950's.

TIME:
The time of the play is about midnight of a night in March, 1959. There is no passage of time except that of the performance. It is obviously late in the evening, and it is equally late in Billie Holiday's life. Four months from now she will die of cirrhosis and heart failure in a hospital in Harlem on Friday, 17 July 1959.

PLAYING TIME:
Depending on how the songs are used, the playing time should be approximately 1 hr., 25 min. It should not exceed 1 hr., 35 minutes.

CHARACTERS

BILLIE HOLIDAY . . . . the great jazz singer in the last
year of her life (age 44).

JIMMY POWERS. . . . . a piano player, any age.

Although other musicians have been used, the play requires only
the two players listed above.

AUTHOR'S NOTE:

Although LADY DAY AT EMERSON'S BAR & GRILL deals
with one of the last appearances of Billie Holiday, the perform-
ances should be "up-beat" in every way. Joy and humor should
be the prevalent emotions felt on stage. This is because singing
was Billie's salvation. Even when she sings a "sad song" her joy
in the act of singing should transform the song into a celebration for the audience. A couple of times she's not able to do this
and she quickly stops the song. There should never be any pain
in the singing itself (except, perhaps, in "Strange Fruit" which
was always a terrible experience for her).

The stories she tells should also be delivered as if they were the
funniest things imaginable. The horror of her life will effect the
audience much more if *she* seems almost oblivious to it herself.
An example is the story of her grandmother's death. She says,
"One mornin' she an' me woke up, see, an' she was dead!" To
Billie, thirty-five years later, this is hilarious. Her next line
about, "That an' bein' raped when I was ten . . ." should also
be tossed off as if they were "nothing" in comparison to what
she went thru during her "cold-turkey" withdrawal. Only
when Billie gets into "what Philly did for me," her revelations
about the trial, her imprisonment, and the denial of her "work
card" and her inability to sing in the clubs, only then should we
see the horror and pain of her life. When the word "heroin" is
used it should be pronounced "hair-on."

Lady Day at Emerson's Bar & Grill

[MUSIC # 1: OVERTURE]

AT RISE: Stage is dark. Over the "live" microphone comes the SOUND of BILLIE'S VOICE.

BILLIE. (*pleading*) No. I told you I can't. I CAN'T DO . . .

(*The microphone is suddenly CUT OFF. Pause. In the dark and over the once-more "live" microphone comes sound of PIANO PLAYER'S VOICE:*)

[MUSIC # 2/3: I'M IN LOVE AGAIN/I WONDER WHERE OUR LOVE HAS GONE]

PIANO PLAYER. (*Off-stage.*) Good evening, Ladies and Gentlemen. Welcome to Philadelphia's liveliest nightspot in south Philly, Emerson's Bar and Grill, with Hal Emerson hisself doing the honors behind the big bar and tonight presenting on the little stage, the legend in her own time, the one and only Lady Day, Miss Billie "GOD BLESS THE CHILD WHAT'S GOT HIS OWN" Holiday.

(*LIGHTS COME UP on BILLIE standing on-stage. Stage-right, in the shadows is an upright piano, behind which sits THE PIANO PLAYER (Jimmy Powers). If other pieces of a combo are used, they would be still further stage-right.*
BILLIE HOLIDAY is in the last year of her life. It is March, 1959. SHE wears a white satin dress, white high-heels, paste earrings and necklace. On her arms are long, fingerless gloves to hide the scars from a thousand injections into each arm. Her lipstick is bright red. SHE clutches a corsage of white gardenias. Atop the piano is a whiskey glass filled to the brim.
Slightly to stage-left is an old-fashioned microphone on a stationary stand. After a short pause, SHE steps to the microphone. There are two notes played on the piano by the PIANO PLAYER, and BILLIE begins to sing "I WONDER WHERE OUR LOVE HAS GONE." After SHE is an entire line into the song, The accompaniment follows.)

BILLIE. (*singing*)
ALL I KNOW IS I'M IN LOVE WITH YOU
EVEN THOUGH YOU SAY THAT WE ARE THROUGH
I KNOW WITHOUT YOUR LOVE I JUST CAN'T GO ON.
I WONDER WHERE OUR LOVE HAS GONE.
ALWAYS THOUGHT YOU'D LOVE ME MORE AN'
    MORE.
NEVER DREAMED YOU'D EVER LET ME GO.
I KNOW WITHOUT YOUR LOVE I JUST CAN'T GO ON.
I WONDER WHERE OUR LOVE HAS GONE.

OH, WHAT DID I DO AND WHAT DID I SAY
THAT EVER COULD LEAD YOU TO TREAT ME
    THIS WAY?
IF I'VE BEEN UNTRUE I'M WILLING TO PAY,
AND DARLING IF THAT'S NOT ENOUGH I'LL DO
    ANYTHING YOU SAY.

SO, DARLING, PLEASE, WHEREVER YOU MAY BE,
HEAR MY PLEA AND HURRY HOME TO ME.
I KNOW WITHOUT YOUR LOVE I JUST CAN'T GO ON.
I WONDER WHERE OUR LOVE HAS GONE.

OH WHAT DID I DO AND WHAT DID I SAY
THAT EVER COULD LEAD YOU TO TREAT ME
    THIS WAY?
IF I'VE BEEN UNTRUE I'M WILLING TO PAY,
AND DARLING IF THAT'S NOT ENOUGH I'LL DO
    ANYTHING YOU SAY.

SO DARLING PLEASE, WHEREVER YOU MAY BE,
HEAR MY PLEA AND HURRY BACK TO ME.
I KNOW WITHOUT YOUR LOVE I JUST CAN'T GO ON.
I WONDER WHERE OUR LOVE HAS GONE.
I WONDER WHERE OUR LOVE HAS GONE.

(*When SHE finishes without even waiting for applause, SHE
    sings "WHEN A WOMAN LOVES A MAN."*)

[MUSIC # 4: WHEN A WOMAN LOVES A MAN]

BILLIE. (*singing*)
MAYBE HE'S NOT MUCH, JUST ANOTHER MAN

DOIN' WHAT HE CAN.
BUT WHAT DOES SHE CARE, WHEN A WOMAN
    LOVES A MAN?
SHE'LL JUST STRING ALONG ALL THROUGH
    THICK AND THIN
TILL HIS SHIP COMES IN.
IT'S ALWAYS THAT WAY WHEN A WOMAN LOVES
    A MAN.

SHE'LL BE THE FIRST ONE TO PRAISE HIM WHEN
    HE'S GOIN' STRONG,
THE LAST ONE TO BLAME HIM WHEN
    EVERYTHING'S WRONG.
IT'S SUCH A ONE-SIDED GAME THAT THEY PLAY,
BUT WOMEN ARE FUNNY THAT WAY.

TELL HER SHE'S A FOOL, SHE'LL SAY, "YES, I
    KNOW, BUT I LOVE HIM SO,"
AND THAT'S HOW IT GOES WHEN A WOMAN
    LOVES A MAN.

SHE'LL BE THE FIRST ONE TO PRAISE HIM WHEN
    HE'S GOIN' STRONG,
THE LAST ONE TO BLAME HIM WHEN
    EVERYTHING'S WRONG.
IT'S SUCH A ONE-SIDED GAME THAT THEY PLAY,
BUT WOMEN ARE FUNNY THAT WAY.

TELL HER SHE'S A FOOL, SHE'LL SAY, "YES, I
    KNOW, BUT I LOVE HIM SO,"
AND THAT'S HOW IT GOES WHEN A WOMAN
    LOVES A MAN.

BILLIE. Thank you. So much. I love it. (*SHE laughs.*) You
know that. Love it. Makes me feel good. I'm even glad to be back
in Philly and that's somethin' for me. You know that. Philly's
been the rat's ass for me. Shit. I used to tell everybody when I die I
don't care if I go to Heaven or Hell long's it ain't in Philly. But I
love singin' here at Emerson's Bar again. It's great. I love it.
Emerson and me is ol' drinkin' buddies, ain't we, Em? We go all
the way back to the bad ol' days. Em give me these flowers. I used
to couldn't sing 'less I had flowers in my damn head. An' they had
to be gardenias. Em never forgot that. No matter how tough
things got. So ever'time I come to Philly, Em'd have a box of 'em

for me. Over there behind the bar. I didn't put 'em on tonight, Em, 'cause I'm the new Billie now. An' I don't need flowers. D.J.'s always talkin' on the radio 'bout the NEW Billie as opposed to the OLD Billie. Said I should change my name to Lady YES-TERday. What they want's the old Billie. That's a crock. Nobody's gettin' any younger. Leastways nobody I know. Shit. But they gotta make a livin' too. I don't care. I just wanna sing. That's all. But they won't let me sing in New York, see, an' singin' in a nice small club like this? There's nothin' like it. Not all the big bands or nothin's so nice as this. Just like I was home an' all of you was my friends. Know what I mean? I love to sing. Singin' is livin' to me, an' they won't let me.

[MUSIC # 4A: UNDERSCORE]

(*PIANO PLAYER begins playing introduction to "WHAT A LITTLE MOONLIGHT CAN DO." BILLIE continues talking while he plays:*)

Oh, I want to introduce my accompanist, Mr. Jimmy Powers at piano. See, a singer's accompanist is home. That's where she finds all the fields to roam through the song in, see. Jimmy here is so important to me. He's my main man, ain't you Jimmy? He's shy. We been together a long time. This week's our anniversary. Five damn months. Takes care of me. Sees I got my shoes on the right feet, an' my music, an' my dress on straight. All that shit. Keeps me happy. Fixes things for me so they're okay when they get so bad, don't you, Jimmy? Gives me a little moonlight when I need it, don't you Jimmy?

(*At this point SHE awaits her lyric for the song which PIANO PLAYER has been playing through all of the above. BILLIE sings: "WHAT A LITTLE MOONLIGHT CAN DO."*)

[MUSIC # 5: WHAT A LITTLE MOONLIGHT CAN DO]

BILLIE. (*singing*)
OOO, OOO, OOO, WHAT A LITTLE MOONLIGHT
CAN DO.
OOO, WHAT A LITTLE MOONLIGHT CAN DO TO YOU.
YOU'RE IN LOVE, YOUR HEART'S AFLUTTER AN'
ALL DAY LONG YOU ONLY STUTTER 'CAUSE

YOUR POOR SOUL JUST COULD NOT UTTER THE
  WORDS: I LOVE YOU.

OOO, OOO, OOO, WHAT A LITTLE MOONLIGHT
  CAN DO.
WAIT AWHILE TILL A LITTLE MOONBEAM COMES
  PEEKIN' THROUGH.
YOU'LL GET SO, YOU CAN'T RESIST HIM AND
ALL YOU'LL SAY WHEN YOU HAVE KISSED HIM IS
OOO, WHAT A LITTLE MOONLIGHT CAN DO.

OOO, OOO, OOO, WHAT A LITTLE MOONLIGHT
  CAN DO.
OOO, WHAT A LITTLE MOONLIGHT CAN DO TO YOU.
YOU'RE IN LOVE, YOUR HEART'S AFLUTTER AN'
ALL DAY LONG YOU ONLY STUTTER 'CAUSE
YOUR POOR SOUL JUST COULD NOT UTTER THE
  WORDS: I LOVE YOU.

OOO, OOO, OOO, WHAT A LITTLE MOONLIGHT
  CAN DO
WAIT AWHILE TILL A LITTLE MOONBEAM COMES
  PEEKIN' THROUGH.
YOU'LL GET SO, YOU CAN'T RESIST HIM AND
ALL YOU'LL SAY WHEN YOU HAVE KISSED HIM IS
OOO, WHAT A LITTLE MOONLIGHT CAN DO.

BILLIE. Ain't that the truth? Jimmy gives me my moonlight, don't you Jimmy? When I need it? Jimmy, why you sit over there in the dark for anyway? He's not mad. He's just shy. Don't want to be seen with no jailbird. Naw, I'm kiddin'. He's alright. See, we got this contract which says I got to sing so many songs a night, see, and some of 'em has to be certain ones you all want to hear like "STRANGE FRUIT" and "GOD BLESS THE CHILD" and all that damn shit. But I'm not like that, see. I got to sing the way I feel. I got to sort of roam around awhile and find the song — or more like let the song find me. That's why Jimmy's so good. He keeps me in line and sees I sing all the numbers I'm supposed to. Before I get too far juiced. Last year . . . no, year before. Spring of '57 I done sing all night in a little bar outside Baltimore, my ol' home town, then some horse's butt tell me he ain't payin' nothin' because I didn't sing "GOD BLESS THE CHILD" or some shit like that. An' I didn't because of my mom, see. I wrote that damn song for her an' it always make me think of her, and that night just happen to be the same date as the day she died an' I flat-ass couldn't sing it. In this country you better move on your pocket book instead of on your feelin's sweetheart or you're gonna find youself way up shit's creek without no paddle. I sung in a club in Harlem once for six or seven hours and they told me my drinks was all they was payin' me. But that was right after I come out of prison. An' that wasn't even a white man did that. That's why it's so nice singin' at Emerson's. Em's home to me. We're ol' drinkin' buddies, ain't we, Em? He married the sweetest bitch I ever met. Next to the Duchess. That was my Mom.

(*PIANO PLAYER starts playing "CRAZY HE CALLS ME."
BILLIE begins singing almost automatically, but stops after
singing only the following.*)

[MUSIC # 6: CRAZY HE CALLS ME]

BILLIE. (*singing*)
I SAY I'LL MOVE THE MOUNTAIN AND I'LL MOVE
    THE MOUNTAIN IF HE WANTS IT OUT OF THE WAY.
CRAZY HE CALLS ME. SURE I'M CRAZY. CRAZY
    IN LOVE I'D SAY.

(*Though SHE stops singing, PIANO PLAYER continues playing
for a time, thinking SHE might re-join him.*)

BILLIE. I'm not supposed to tell it, but Jimmy an' me is goin' to get married. As soon as my next divorce comes through. Ain't we, Jimmy? But he don't want me tellin' anybody. See, all I ever wanted was a beautiful home and some kids. Even just the kids. I love kids an' I never had any. Not even one.
    BILLIE. (*singing*)
LIKE THE WIND THAT SHAKES THE BOUGH, HE
    MOVES ME WITH A SMILE
THE DIFFICULT I'D DO RIGHT NOW. THE
    IMPOSSIBLE WILL TAKE A LITTLE WHILE.

I SAY I'LL CARE FOREVER AND I MEAN FOREVER
IF I HAVE TO HOLD UP THE SKY
CRAZY HE CALLS ME—SURE I'M CRAZY, CRAZY
    IN LOVE AM I.

BILLIE. An' I want lots an' lots of kids. If I only coulda had me some kids I . . . I never would have . . . I'd never have got into no trouble. I'm sure of it. It's what I used to tell Sonny. Sonny Monroe, my first love. He wasn't my best, but he was my first. He was the worst one I ever had too. We was married but he didn't want no kids. Crazy he called me. But Sonny don't know Emerson's, do you, Sonny? I mean, Jimmy. He don't know, does he, Em? They used to be hangin' from the rafters in this place to see me in those days. I was hot shit. See, the disc jockey's say I'm not the same Lady Day, but what they don't know is you can only get to where you're at by the way of where you been. It don't matter if it's good or bad, you wouldn't be what or who you are now if you hadn't been whatever you was way back when. See, I KNOW who I am now is because of who I was THEN. What I am an' what I was come from wantin' Louis' feelin' and Bessie Smith's big sound. For the longest time imaginable that's all I was, was that longin' walkin' round on two legs. (*laughs*) When I was a stupid-ass kid in Baltimore I scrubbed the steps to the local fancy house run by a big ass woman named Alice Dean. She wore these humongus red velvet hats with bird-of-paradise feathers, see, so I wanted to buy one of those hats for the Duchess. That was my Mom. I didn't know those hats was kind of a walking advertise-ment for bitches who was sellin' it. (*laughs*) Mom didn't know that either. She wasn't too much older'n me an' she wasn't a hell of a lot smarter neither. She never did get more'n five feet tall and weighed eighty pounds while I was over 200 pounds by the time I was twelve. So we was pals like I was her sister. But at Alice Dean's house, see, I got to play these records till I practically wore them all out. Also that damn ol' wind-up victrola which was the only kind they had anywhere's in those days. That was about 1922 or three or so. See, at Miss Dean's Parlor and Entertainment Estab-lishment the girls there was half colored. Whore houses or sportin' houses as they was called was the only place white folks and coloreds could meet. They sure wasn't allowed to meet in no church. And all those bitches at Miss Dean's cat house had all these damn Louis Armstrong records and Bessie Smith records and I was gassin' my fat ass out playin' 'em. That's when I started to sing. Was listenin' to those records. Especially listenin' to Pops. That's what we all called Louis Armstrong was Pops. He had this one song called "West Side Blues" and he'd go, "oh bee doh, oh bee doh-ee-doh," and I'd wonder why he didn't sing any words, and he'd have the most beautiful feelin' and I wanted that feelin'. And I also wanted Bessie's big sound, but my voice wasn't big like that, so between the two of them I sort of got Billie Holiday. But Pops Armstrong and Bessie Smith on the victrola was sort of Mom and Pop to me.

(*PIANO PLAYER plays lead-in to "CRAZY HE CALLS ME."*)

BILLIE. Aw, come on, Jimmy. Don't pull that shit. These is my friends. (*PIANO PLAYER stops immediately.*) Jimmy's afraid I'm gonna get on a cryin' jag or somethin'. I'm not, Jimmy. I'm happy. (*singing:*) "Ooo, Ooo, Ooo. What a little moonlight can doooo!" Relax, Jimmy. I'm okay. But I'm gonna be needin' a little moonlight before too long, so don't get your hopes up! That's what has Jimmy so upset. He worries about me. He gets so pissed with me. You know why? He has this notion that I'm better'n he is. Cause I'm the star, see. And that I oughta behave in some kinda unnatural ways. Or ways that is naturally superior. Shit. I know that ain't so. I told him that. I didn't travel through the South for nothin!. I know nobody's better'n anybody else. Less you're colored. Then you're better'n everybody. (*laughs*) No, I'm only kiddin'. I knew a nice white person. Once! (*laughs*) No. They're just like us. Only meaner. I'm kiddin'. Listen, honey. We all put on our drawers the same way: one leg at a time. There's only one main difference between the ofays and us colored. All our black's on the OUTside. (*laughs*) Somebody sayin' they're better than you don't make it so. No way, José! Nobody's better'n you are 'less you THINK they are. I been through all that shit. Shit. Ever fuckin' nigger who's ever been called a Nigger knows that. (*laughs*) Shit. I been through that shit. (*to PIANO PLAYER:*) How come you sit over there in the dark? How can you play in that dark? I can't. I need light. I want light. Music is light to me. Come on, Jimmy. Give us a Bessie number. Give us a little "PIG'S FOOT."

[MUSIC # 7: PIGS FOOT]

BILLIE. (*singing*)
UP IN HARLEM EVER SATURDAY NIGHT
WHEN THE HIGHBROWS GET TOGETHER IT'S
    JUST TOO BRIGHT
THEY ALL CONGREGATE AN' ALL-NIGHT HOP
AND WHAT THEY DO IS BOP-A-DOP.
OL' HANNAH BROWN FROM WAY CROSS TOWN

GETS FULL OF CORN
AND STARTS BRINGIN 'EM DOWN
AND AT THE BREAK OF DAY YOU CAN HEAR OL'
  HANNAH SAY:

GIVE ME A PIG'S FOOT AND A BOTTLE OF BEER
SEND ME JAKE, I DON'T CARE
I FEEL JUST LIKE I WANNA CLOWN
GIVE THE PIANA PLAYER A DRINK BECAUSE HE'S
  BRINGIN' ME DOWN.
HE'S GOT RHYTHM—YEAH—WHEN HE STOMPS
  HIS FEET
HE SENDS ME RIGHT OFF TO SLEEP
CHECK ALL YOUR RAZORS AND YOUR GUN
WE'RE GONNA BE ARRESTED WHEN THE WAGON
  COMES
GIVE ME A PIG'S FOOT AND A BOTTLE OF BEER
SEND ME CAUSE I DON'T CARE.

GIVE ME A PIG'S FOOT AND A BOTTLE OF BEER
SEND ME JAKE, I DON'T CARE
I FEEL JUST LIKE A WANTA CLOWN
GIVE THE PIANA PLAYER A DRINK BECAUSE HE'S
  BRINGIN' ME DOWN.
HE'S GOT RHYTHM—YEAH—WHEN HE STOMPS
  HIS FEET

HE MOVE ME RIGHT OFF TO SLEEP
CHECK ALL YOUR RAZORS AND YOUR GUN
WE'RE GONNA BE ARRESTED WHEN THE WAGON
  COMES
GIVE ME A PIG'S FOOT AND A BOTTLE OF BEER
SEND ME CAUSE I DON'T CARE
SEND ME CAUSE I DON'T CARE.

(BILLIE begins talking even though the song is not over and
    PIANO PLAYER continues playing through the end of the
    number.)

BILLIE. I love those damn pig's feet, an' I cook 'em good, too. I
boil 'em and then bake 'em in a real hot oven 'til they crisp as
potato chips, an' then put barbeque sauce on 'em. Umm. Them
and red beans is my favorite. My Mom, the Duchess, taught me

how to cook. That was the early thirties. Bessie was makin' her records then too, but I never met her. I came close though. She cut her last set of records just three days before I cut my first. See, a few of the songs I sing have the twelve-bar blues beat, but I'm not a blues singer like Bessie. I never was. I'm a jazz singer. What I do is the blues feeling with the jazz beat. When I started to sing with the dance bands nobody paid attention to the singer 'cause the vocal wasn't important. It was the band that was everything. I only sang one chorus and it wasn't the first. The horns had that. That's how all my records with Teddy Wilson's Band was made. And even with Artie Shaw. That's why toward the end of the thirties I started my own damn band was so I could get to sing the lyrics. I wanted to sing, see. I had to. Singin's always been the best part of livin' to me. But they wouldn't let us coloreds record the first or second rated songs. What the big ass record companies thought was going to be the hits was all saved for the grays. The white folks, in case you're wonderin'. Teddy Wilson asked me to cut some sides 'cause he heard me singin' for tips in a little place up in Harlem called the Hot Cha Bar. So we made some songs nobody'd ever heard of, cause colored couldn't cut any of the really big songs. That's why Bessie Smith made all those songs nobody ever head of, 'cause her fat old ass was too black to get to sing any ofay songs.

[MUSIC # 8: BABY DOLL]

(*Now BILLIE starts singing a song the PIANO PLAYER doesn't seem to know, though HE tries to improvise an accompaniment about half-way through. It is "BABY DOLL" — one of Bessie Smith's.*)

BILLIE. (*singing*)
HONEY, THERE'S A FUNNY FEELIN' ROUND MY
    HEART
AND IT'S BOUND TO DRIVE YOUR MOMMA WILD.
IT MUST BE SOMETHIN' THEY CALL THE CUBAN DIVE.
IT'S WON YOUR MOMMA, ANGEL CHILD.
I WENT TO SEE THE DOCTOR THE OTHER DAY.
HE SAID I'S WELL AS WELL COULD BE.
BUT I SAID. "DOCTOR, YOU DON'T KNOW REALLY
    WHAT'S WORRYIN' ME.
I WANNA BE SOMEBODY'S BABY DOLL, SO'S

I CAN GET MY LOVIN' ALL THE TIME.
I WANNA BE SOMEBODY'S BABY DOLL, EASE MY
  MIND.
HE CAN BE UGLY. HE CAN BE BLACK,
SO LONG'S HE GIVE ME THE ROCKIN' BALL AN' JACK!"
I WANNA BE SOMEBODY'S BABY DOLL, SO'S I CAN GET
MY LOVIN' ALL THE TIME, I MEAN,
TO GET MY LOVIN' ALL THE TIME.

BILLIE. (*laughs*) Shit like that. Bessie was somethin' else. (*laughs*) But I got to watch myself here, 'cause they got what's called the parole officers and if they see me havin' myself too good a time they're liable to think I broke mine. If that happens these dudes'll jump on me like I don't know what. You can always spot 'em too. They always come to one of the late shows, like this one. An' they always come in late. They wanna make sure I'm not havin' too much fun. They don't want coloreds to have much fun, might start gettin' too uppity or somethin'. An' they always white. I don't think any coloreds work for the government. I guess not enough of us voted for Mr. Eisenhower. Anyway, they're always white, they always come late, and they always wear these damn white socks. Now you watch 'em later when they come in and see if they don't. I don't know why that is. Maybe a government resolution against colored socks. I don't know. For some reason they seem scared of colored folks and colored socks. Anyway. If I sudden start singin' "Baby Get Lost" you'll know they here. Then you don't know what'll happen, do you, Jimmy? Anything can happen, can't it, Jimmy? (*singing:*) "We gonna be arrested when the wagon comes. Give me a pig's foot and a bottle of beer. Send me cause I don't care." In this country bein' arrested is the colored folks tradition. Since the ofays set us free, they don't know what to do with us but lock us up! I never come to Philly but they. . . . Okay. Okay, Jimmy over there's givin' me the fish eye, so I better cut out some of this shit and pay attention to the man. But it's not my fault, Jimmy. It's bein' back here in Philly. You knew that when you set this whole thing up. See, I never got on too well in Philly. All the white mens in the blue suits with the brass buttons and they white socks is always bustin' my ass whenever I come to Philly. I been arrested all over the country but Philly's the only place ever made me a candidate for federal housing. Okay, Jimmy. Okay. He wants me to sing a song for you I wrote for my Mom, the Duchess. She wasn't no real Duchess of course, 'cause we don't got any black or colored Duchess. Not in this world. But my good buddie, Prez, that's Lester Young on the tenor sax, I called him Prez, 'cause to me he's the president of saxophone players. Well, he called my mom the Duchess. He said since I was Lady Day, an' he's the one who give me that name, see we just took a time for namin' everybody: he name me, I named him, he name my Mom. (*laughs*) Well he said the Mom of a Lady must gotta be a Duchess. Well Mom just loved it. She never had liked her name, which was Sadie Fagan, so who could blame her? And I was Eleanora Fagan. So you see right off what we was up against. So after the Prez call her "Duchess" then everybody did. At first you call her Duchess she light up like a Christmas tree, but then she come to expect it ever damn time you speak to her. Finally you didn't call her that she'd think you some kinda damn nigger, an' practic'ly everybody knew the Duchess. All my friends an' close to all Harlem, too. She ran an open house and open kitchen for ever damn down an' out somebody she met. An' you didn't have to be anybody to be somebody to the Duchess. She was the soul of generosity, except for one time when Sonny Monroe an' me was down an' just about goin' for the count, an' I ask her for help an' she tell me no, after all the help I give her, openin' her restaurant an' all that, an she said no. Not as long as I was with Sonny, she said. Wouldn't help me, she said. We was bad, too. We needed help in the worst way. Needed a little moonlight. Maybe just a moonbeam or two. Anything. An' the duchess said no. Said Sonny was the only colored man she ever seen who was blacker on the inside than on the out. She told me he'd ruin my life. Said he was no good for nothin' but greasin' my runway to hell. Said the stuff he was on had stolen her baby Billie. Said my sweet soul was not my own an' she was right. The Duchess was always right. What she didn't know was how sweet he was to me. Little Sonny. He was my first love, an' my worst love. He was just like a little boy, all scared an' helpless. That's all. He didn't mean bad. Not in his heart. (*singing*) "Tell her she's a fool. She'll say 'Yes, I know, but I love him so!' An' that's how it is when a woman loves a man." (*laughs*) So we moved out. Sonny Monroe an' me. An' I wrote her this song. An' it always made her mad 'cause she knew I wrote it for her. She knew.

[MUSIC # 9: GOD BLESS THE CHILD]

(*PIANO PLAYER plays "GOD BLESS THE CHILD THAT'S GOT HIS OWN." BILLIE sings it.*)

BILLIE. (*singing*)
THEM THAT'S GOT SHALL GET
THEM THAT'S NOT SHALL LOSE,
SO THE BIBLE SAY
AND IT STILL IS NEWS.
MAMA MAY HAVE, PAPA MAY HAVE
BUT GOD BLESS THE CHILD THAT'S GOT HIS OWN.

YES, THE STRONG GETS MORE
WHILE THE WEAK ONES FADE.
EMPTY POCKETS DON'T EVER MAKE THE GRADE.
MAMA MAY HAVE, PAPA MAY HAVE
BUT GOD BLESS THE CHILD THAT'S GOT HIS OWN,
THAT'S GOT HIS OWN.

MONEY, YOU GOT LOTS OF FRIENDS
CROWDIN' ROUND YOUR DOOR.
BUT WHEN YOU'RE GONE AND SPENDIN' ENDS,
THEY DON'T COME NO MORE.

RICH RELATIONS GIVE
CRUST OF BREAD AND SUCH
YOU CAN HELP YOURSELF
BUT DON'T TAKE TOO MUCH.
MAMA MAY HAVE, PAPA MAY HAVE
BUT GOD BLESS THE CHILD THAT'S GOT HIS OWN
THAT'S GOT HIS OWN.
ETC.

BILLIE. That was for my Mom, the Duchess, cause I love her still. Even if she is dead an' told me no. Nobody but me ever liked Sonny. I was all he had. That was why I stopped seein' my best friend Prez was because he tried to get me off the stuff. Told me Sonny Monroe was no good. Told me Sonny was into stuff that'll eat up your life. But I loved the man, see. He was my man. Like my own little manchild. My little sweetie. I didn't know 'bout heroin an' all that shit. Not really. Not before Sonny. The Duchess used to say my best talent was for pickin' the rottenest apple in the bunch, an' poor black little skinny Sonny Monroe took the cake for her. She never had truck with no one 'cept Pop and one longshoreman in Baltimore after she an' Pop got divorced. But the longshoreman died and after that she had no use for any man an' especially not for any of mine. Her daddy's mama was a slave owned body and soul by a big, red-headed Irish dude who owned the plantation. That was my great granny, see. She had sixteen kids by that man an' he was where we got the name Fagin. I loved that old woman an' used to sleep with her ever night in Baltimore when I was eight or nine an' she was some more'n ninety-six. An' she'd wrap her skinny old arms around me so tight like she was scared of sleepin' by herself or of the dark or somethin'. An' one morning, see, she an' me woke up an' she was dead, an' the neighbors come in 'cause they heard me screamin' the house down an' I had to go to the hospital for a month. I loved her, see, but she was dead an' spookin' me out. I never forget that. That an' bein' raped when I was ten was almost the worst things that ever happened to me. They wasn't, but they come damn close. (*She laughs.*) So whenever the Duchess'd get too uppitty with me I'd just say, "How white of you" 'cause she had all this white blood in her 'cause of this Irish dude Fagin as her grand daddy, see, and that always made her hoppin' mad. (*laughs*) When she married my Pop she was only sixteen. He was only eighteen an' I was only three. My Pop died in '37, same year as Bessie Smith. He played guitar with McKinney's Cotton Pickers and later with Fletcher Henderson's touring band. He always wanted to sing, see, but before he got to do that, he got sent to fight in the First World War. The one they said was the war to end all war, but the only thing it seem to end was my Pop's singin' career 'cause his lungs was burned out by gas in the trenches in France. So, I never heard Pop sing, but the Duchess said before the war he had the sweetest sound you could ever hear on a man. That was what killed him, too. That an' being colored. Just like Bessie. He didn't have his arm cut off like her in no car crash an' bleed to death before they could find a white hospital that'd admit colored, but it was the same, really. Because his lungs was so bad, a chest cold for him was terrible, an' while he was travellin' through Texas with the band he got this little chest cold an' they couldn't find no doctor'd see no colored, an' course there weren't no such thing as a colored doctor. So by the time they got him to the Veteran's Hospital in Dallas where they had to take him 'cause he was a veteran even if he was colored, it was too late anyhow. An' I was singin' up at the Hot Cha Bar in Harlem. An' they call me to the phone for this long-distance call for Miss Eleanora Billie Holiday Fagan and that was sort of my name because I had been born Eleanora Fagan and I used Billie because my favorite movie star was Billie Dove, see, and I'd seen all her pictures and even wore my hair like she did, so I said, "Yes," into that wall phone with all the numbers and people's initials an' all that shit scratched into it. I said, "Yes, this is me," and this strange voice I'd never heard before from far away somewhere's where I couldn't even imagine said my daddy was dead and what did I want done with the remains. Just like that. What did I want done with the remains. An' I didn't say a word. Just hung up the receiver so quiet an' still they musta thought it was a disconnect. An' I went back on-stage to sing. An' I did, because . . . because I . . . I . . .

[MUSIC # 9A: FOOLIN MYSELF]

(*PIANO PLAYER plays the long intro to "FOOLIN' MYSELF" which allows BILLIE to come back from the long distance phone call. SHE sees the piano, the bar, the people, recognizes the song and sings the closing chorus.*)

BILLIE. (*singing*)
AND EVERY TIME I PASS AND SEE MYSELF IN
    THE LOOKING GLASS
I TIP MY HAT AND SAY, "HOW DO YOU DO,
    FOOL? YOU'VE THROWN YOUR LIFE AWAY."
I'M ACTING GAY, I'M ACTING PROUD
AND EVERY TIME I SEE YOU IN A CROWD,
I MAKE PRETEND, BUT IN THE END
I'M JUST FOOLIN' MYSELF.
    BILLIE. Jimmy. "SOMEBODY'S ON MY MIND."

[MUSIC # 10: SOMEBODY'S ON MY MIND]

(*PIANO PLAYER plays "SOMEBODY'S ON MY MIND." BILLIE sings it.*)

BILLIE. (*singing*)
SOMEBODY'S ON MY MIND
LIKE AN OLD SWEET SONG THAT'S LOST IN TIME.
SOMEBODY'S ON MY MIND, SO I'M WALKIN' ON
    CLOUDS ALL SILVER-LINED.
TO DREAM MY DREAM COULD BE MY MISTAKE
BUT I'D RATHER BE WRONG AND SLEEP RIGHT
    ALONG THAN WAKE.
LOVE MAY BE BLIND, I'LL TAKE MY CHANCE

THAT IF HE CARES THIS AFFAIR IS A REAL ROMANCE,
THAT'S WHY YOU'LL FIND
SOMEBODY'S ON MY MIND.

TO DREAM MY DREAM COULD BE MY MISTAKE
BUT I'D RATHER BE WRONG AND SLEEP RIGHT
    ALONG THAN WAKE.
LOVE MAY BE BLIND, I'LL TAKE MY CHANCE
THAT HE CARES THIS AFFAIR'S MY REAL ROMANCE.
THAT'S WHY YOU'LL FIND
SOMEBODY'S ON MY MIND.

BILLIE. Jimmy. I'm not doin' so good here, Jimmy.
PIANO PLAYER. Lady. You all right.
BILLIE. I'm not doin' so good here, Jimmy. I need a little help,
now Jimmy.
PIANO PLAYER. Don't say that. You're doin' fine, Lady Day.
You doin' fine. How 'bout some good time songs, Lady? How
'bout "EASY LIVIN'"?

[MUSIC # 11: EASY LIVIN]

(*PIANO PLAYER plays "EASY LIVIN'." BILLIE sings "EASY
    LIVIN'."*)

BILLIE. (*singing*)
LIVING FOR YOU IS EASY LIVIN'
IT'S EASY TO LIVE WHEN YOU'RE IN LOVE
AND I'M SO IN LOVE. THERE'S NOTHING IN LIFE
    BUT YOU.
I'LL NEVER REGRET THE YEARS I'M GIVING.
IT'S EASY TO GIVE WHEN YOU'RE IN LOVE.
SO I'M HAPPY TO DO WHATEVER I DO FOR YOU.

FOR YOU, BABY, I'M A FOOL BUT IT'S FUN.
PEOPLE SAY YOU RULE ME WITH ONE WAVE OF
    YOUR HAND
DARLING, IT'S GRAND. THEY JUST DON'T
    UNDERSTAND.
LIVING FOR YOU IS EASY LIVING.
IT'S EASY LIVING WHEN YOU'RE IN LOVE

I'M SO IN LOVE THERE'S NOTHING IN LIFE BUT YOU.

FOR YOU, BABY, I'M A FOOL BUT IT'S FUN.
PEOPLE SAY YOU RULE ME WITH ONE WAVE OF
   YOUR HAND
DARLING, IT'S GRAND. THEY JUST DON'T
   UNDERSTAND.
LIVING FOR YOU IS EASY LIVING
IT'S EASY LIVING WHEN YOU'RE IN LOVE
I'M SO IN LOVE THERE'S NOTHING IN LIFE BUT YOU.

BILLIE. Easy livin'. Like the times I was singin' with Artie's band. Artie Shaw. An' we toured, see. We started out in Boston an' it was all down hill from that. In Boston, see, I had to sit in the bus till it was time for my numbers 'cause they didn't want no black bitch sittin' up on the bandstand with all those fellahs in the band which was all-white, see, so you can imagine when we got down to Virginia, North an' South Carolina. Georgia. An' worse. Anyway, there was this fancy restaurant we went into outside of Birmingham an' Artie an' the boys just couldn't have been sweeter or squarer with me. Places where they wouldn't let me in the front door none of them'd use the front door neither. An' if I had to sit out in the kitchen to get some eats the whole bunch of them'd sit out there too. So that always pissed off the ofays who ran the places anyway, see. So this one place we went to we was all sittin' out in the kitchen with all the colored help runnin' around us tryin' to do their jobs in that place just like we wasn't there. An' it was hot as hell in that kitchen anyway, and of course none of this treatment was free you know. We was all payin' top price for this, just like we was sittin' out front with all the grays. Only we was in the kitchen because Artie Shaw had this black bitch called Billie Holiday in his troupe. So everything was smooth as silk till I realized all of a sudden I had to use the bathroom in the worst way. I mean, my kidneys was almost to bust an' float me outta there right into the main dining room, an' I knew damn well they didn't want that. So I got up an' asked this black dude who looked like he might have had some sense where was the bathroom an' he asked me why I wanted to know, thereby provin' he didn't have any more sense than I had in askin'. I shoulda found it on my own. Anyway, while I was tryin' to explain to him that I didn't really need to go there to powder my nose, if that's what was worryin' him. That it was for a more essential reason than that, when this blond bitch comes in the kitchen from the dining room. Somebody musta heard me askin' this dude an' run off to get this bitch to bring her into the discussion. Now, she was the maitresse dee who wouldn't let me into the dining room to begin with. So she saunters up real big, still clutchin' all these big red plush covered menus under her left tit and says, "Just what exactly seems to be the trouble here?" an' I look at her, see, like where'd the fuck she come from an' go "The trouble seem to be that this dude can't answer a simple question." So then I knew somebody had ran to get her 'cause she says, "I'm sorry, Miss Day, but we don't have toilets for the colored." An' I said, "Listen, honey, you have me confused. I'm not Doris Day. I'm Billie Holiday. Lots of folks has said she an' me resembles each other, but this is the first time I know of where anybody's talked to the one an' thought they was talkin' to the other. Also I don't want to cast no aspersions on anybody workin' here or hurt anybody's feelin's or nothin' but ever body I see workin' here 'cept you is about as colored as they come. Now, where do they go?" So she gives me this sweet little smile out of one side her mouth an' says, "Yes, but they're males. We don't have a toilet for colored females." I said, "Honey, at this point I don't care if it's nothin' but a urinal or a dark corner of the room. Lead me to it, please. I'm about to bust." So she shifts her weight around slow, see, in this real tight black sequin-covered dress she's wearin' with sequin high-heel shoes to match an' tells me, "We didn't want you comin' in our restaurant to start with. We don't allow colored here. We only let you in because Mr. Shaw agreed to pay twice as much for all of you if we'd let you eat out here in the kitchen. Otherwise you wouldn't even be here. Now, if Mr. Shaw wants to do that, that's his business. But he said nothing about letting you use the phone, or the bar, or the dining room or the men's toilet, and I'm not going to let you do that." So I said, "Listen, Mr. Shaw's been very sweet. He's done a lot of nice things like this for me, and I appreciate it. But one thing I know of he can't do for me and that's piss. So what do you propose I do about this situation?" An' she give me that sweet little twisted side of her mouth smile and clutched a firm grip on that stack of menus and said, "Why don't you sit on it!" I was so shocked. I just looked at her a minute and then I said, "No. I think I'll let you do that." An' I cut loose the biggest deluge all acrossed those sequined shoes of hers to come down the pike since Noah. You never seen a grown woman leap so high up in the air as she did in your life. Droppin' menus and screechin' like she'd been scalded all over the legs and feet by molten lead. An' all the boys in the band was on their feet a jumpin' up and down and hooting an carryin' on like we just won the second coming of the Civil War an' that was I assure you the high an' low of the whole tour for me. After that everybody in the band started sayin' "Watch out for Billie. She's got a secret weapon. She'll spoil your shoes quicker'n you can pay to get 'em polished" an' all kinda silly shit like that. But I loved 'em. They was pals to this black bitch an' I'll never forget it.

[MUSIC # 12: STRANGE FRUIT]

(*PIANO PLAYER plays lead-in to "STRANGE FRUIT." BIL-LIE sings it.*)

BILLIE. (*singing*)
SOUTHERN TREES BEAR A STRANGE FRUIT
BLOOD ON THE LEAVES, AND BLOOD AT THE ROOT.
BLACK BODIES SWINGIN' IN THE SOUTHERN BREEZE
STRANGE FRUIT HANGIN' FROM THE POPLAR TREE.

PASTORAL SCENE OF THE GALLANT SOUTH:
THE BULGING EYES AND THE TWISTED MOUTH
SCENT OF MAGNOLIAS, SWEET AND FRESH,
THEN THE SUDDEN SMELL OF BURNIN' FLESH.
HERE IS A FRUIT FOR THE CROWS TO PLUCK
FOR THE TRAIN TO GATHER
FOR THE WIND TO SUCK
FOR THE SUN TO ROT
FOR THE TREES TO DROP.
HERE IS A STRANGE AND BITTER CROP.

(*Afterwards, SHE seems distraught and begins wandering about the stage.*)

BILLIE. Jimmy? It's bad again, Jimmy. Real bad. Where's my flowers? I need my flowers, Jimmy!
PIANO PLAYER. Lady, here's your flowers.
BILLIE. I can't sing without . . . without my damn flowers, Sonny. I can't.
PIANO PLAYER. Looky here, Lady. Lady!

(*BILLIE Exits. PIANO PLAYER plays over.*) Ladies and gentle-men. Lady Day'll be back after we take a little break. It's been a kind of a long day for Lady. We drove down here early this afternoon all the way from New York City an' she's had a touch of somethin' so we had the doctor back stage earlier, and he's waitin' there now. Nothin' serious. An' I'm sure she'll be right back after this little break. Now, before I go, if you wouldn't mind, an' for your entertainment all you good folks here at Emerson's tonight, I'd like to play a new number for you. One that Mr. Al Hibbler has made numero uno on the charts.

[MUSIC # 13: BLUES ENTR'ACT]

PIANO PLAYER. Thank you. Thank you so much. An' now I'll just take a little break here an' see what the doctor has to say 'bout Lady Day, an' I'm sure we'll both be back out here in no time at all to sing and play for all you good people here at the very heart of Philadelphia's nightlife, Emerson's Bar & Grill.

(*As PIANO PLAYER is getting up to Exit, BILLIE Enters. The long glove on her left arm has been pulled down about her wrist. SHE has had a shot of heroin and SHE is very high. SHE leads a little chihuahua dog on a leash. SHE staggers to the microphone and starts singing "AIN'T NOBODY'S BUSINESS IF I DO." The PIANO PLAYER hurriedly plays.*)

[MUSIC # 14: T'AINT NOBODY'S BUSINESS]

BILLIE. (*singing*)
THERE AIN'T NOTHIN' I CAN'T DO
OR NOTHIN' I CAN'T SAY
THAT FOLKS DON'T CRITICIZE ME
BUT I'M GOING TO DO JUST AS I WANT TO
NO MATTER WHAT PEOPLE SAY.

IF I SHOULD TAKE A NOTION
TO JUMP INTO THE OCEAN
AIN'T NOBODY'S BUSINESS IF I DO.
IF I GO TO CHURCH ON SUNDAY
THEN CABARET ALL DAY MONDAY
AIN'T NOBODY'S BUSINESS IF I DO.
IF MY MAN AIN'T GOT NO MONEY

AND I SAY TAKE ALL OF MINE, HONEY
AIN'T NOBODY'S BUSINESS IF I DO.
IF I GIVE HIM MY LAST NICKEL
AND IT LEAVES ME IN A PICKLE
AIN'T NOBODY'S BUSINESS IF I DO.
WELL, I'D RATHER MY MAN WOULD HIT ME
THEN FOR HIM TO JUST UP AND QUIT ME
AIN'T NOBODY'S BUSINESS IF I DO.
I SWEAR I WOULDN'T CALL NO COPPER
IF I'M BEAT UP BY MY POPPER
AIN'T NOBODY'S BUSINESS IF I DO.
NOBODY'S BUSINESS, AIN'T NOBODY'S BUSINESS
NOBODY'S BUSINESS IF I DO.

BILLIE. An' that's my total philosophy.

PIANO PLAYER. Lady, I was tellin' these good people we'd take a little break now an' come back after the doctor checked out how you're feelin'. Then we can . . .

BILLIE. Don't pull that phony doctor shit, Sonny. These is my friends here. They know I'm not sick. I seen a world of doctors. An' I'm still a nigger, ain't I? No doctor I met has ever cured me of that, has he? (*SHE holds up the dog.*) I want you to meet Pepi. He's my baby. Ain't you, baby? Ain't he a sweetie? He's my pal. Pepi's the most important member of the troupe. Been with me through thick an' thin. Best pal this bitch ever had, ain't you, Pepi? He us'ly stays back in the dressin' room. He don't like me to sing any of the sad songs, see. He don't like to hear me sad. But I ain't sad no more, Pepi. This ain't no sad song. I wanta sing Pepi's song. It's the one I always sing for him 'cause he's so pretty. Ain't that right, Sonny?

(*BILLIE starts snapping her fingers. THE PIANO PLAYER seems to hesitate.*)

BILLIE. Sonny? Where are my flowers? I can't find my damn flowers, Sonny.

(*The PIANO PLAYER leaves the piano and goes to BILLIE. HE pulls up her left glove and takes the dog, which SHE is in danger of dropping. HE has taken the flowers to her. SHE smiles at them.*)

PIANO PLAYER. Lady, we might want to take a little break about now.

BILLIE. (*Trying to put flowers in her hair.*) You know when I . . . when I first got out of the clammer bunch of friends of mine set up for me to sing in Carnegie Hall where all the big long-hair singers an' orchestras an' all that shit play, see.

(*The PIANO PLAYER takes the dog off-stage. BILLIE fastens the flowers in her hair as HE re-enters. HE sits at the piano.*)

BILLIE. An' . . . an' I never had sing in a place like that. I didn't even know if coloreds could buy a ticket let alone stand up an' sing on the stage. So, anyway, I was so nervous before I went on that my knees started knockin' together, see, and I had on this long dress that went all the way down to the floor so you couldn't see my legs, but I couldn't control my knees an' they was shakin' so bad nobody knew if I was gonna sing or dance. But it was wonderful. Wonderful. Sonny? You over there? Sittin' in the dark?

PIANO PLAYER. It's Jimmy, Lady. Jimmy Powers ticklin' the old ivories. You go backstage with Pepi an' have a short break while I entertain these good folks with a few of the old dance tunes.

(*HE faintly plays the piano as SHE talks through the following:*)

BILLIE. (*Ramblingly, almost incoherently.*) Dance? I ain't never been no dancer, Sonny. You know that. Not since't I was sixteen in Harlem at this house run by a white bitch name Florence Williams. Mom had took me there to be a maid, see, but I knew as soon's I laid eyes on the lamp shades and what they called a "chaise lounge" what my duties was goin' to be, but I didn't say nothin' to Mom because she really thought what this bitch Florence wanted was a maid. So I got the job an' did good because I was the only colored bitch in the place, but it drove me crazy, see, and I just couldn't stand it, an' this one guy hurt me so bad I bled solid for a week, so I dragged myself outta there an' hit ever place on Seventh Avenue between 139th Street an' 133rd, askin' for work. An' I was all set to walk all the way down to the Battery an' jump in if nobody'd hired me when I got to this place called Pod's and Jerry's an' they had a sign in the window sayin' "Dancer Wanted" so I went in an' told 'em I was a great dancer an' I wanted the job. (*laughs*) I musta been a sight 'cause I was more'n 200 pounds an' weak from bleedin' all week an' sick an' tired an' hungry an' ever other damn thing too. So the piano player started to play an' I danced the only two steps I knew which was the time step an' the crossover. Danced 'em over an' over an' the piano player stopped an' asked me to please stop wastin' his time, but he must have felt sorry for me cause he said, "Can you sing?" an' I said, "Sure, but what's that? Ever damn body can sing." So I sang. An' they went crazy. An' after that come Benny Goodman to see me, an' the Apollo where I was so scared on openin' night I stuck the flowers in my hair with the pins still in 'em an' lost so much blood I nearly passed out durin' the intermission, but I didn't 'cause the whole place was screamin' "We want Billie! We want . . . Bill . . . Billie." (*Ramblingly, almost incoherently.*) They was like that at Alderson Prison, too. The girls in there was always callin' for me to sing 'em somethin'. Some of 'em even had my records. They all thought I should cheer 'em up by singin' the blues or jazz or some shit. But I couldn't sing in there. Singin' is how you feel. I couldn't sing in a place like that. In Alderson I was dead a year and a day. You ever hear a dead person singin'? That was what Philly did for me. They told me, my damn agent, plead guilty Billie, you get out on suspended sentence, so I stood flat footed up in front of that judge an' said the one word, "Guilty, your Honor," and they send me cold turkey to Alderson Prison. Being in prison in West Virginia is what's called double redundant. That was about ten or twelve years ago. '47, whenever the hell that was. And I was doin' the bad drugs heavy, see, an' they idea of treatin' a sick colored was to strap you to the bedposts so tight I still got the pains in my wrist and ankles when it comes a storm. But the worst was they didn't tell me about the card they call your cabaret card 'cause you got to have that in order to work in the clubs and it's really supposed to be for the folks who does the kitchen work to show they got no disease and shit like that— but for some damn reason ever damn body got to have one and they call it your work card. Only. Only the mens in the blue suits with the brass buttons and white damn socks is the only ones who can give it to you and if you got a felony even out of state they won't let you earn your daily bread. So they told me that after I got out of my year of hell in West Virginia. An' friends of mine set it up so I could sing in Carnegie Hall, see, but I can't ever sing in no club like this and this is heaven to me. An' I tried then to tell 'em no it ain't me, see. I wasn't even at the hotel. I was here at the club when the policemens broke into the room, an' it was you, Sonny, who put the stuff in my suitcase because you said you couldn't make it to the toilet, so you stashed it all in my suitcase 'cause you thought me bein' Billie Holiday an' all that shit the damn cops wouldn't do nothin' to me, an' they already had a police file on you as long as your dick, so I said, "Okay, Sonny." An' I got my chauffeur to drive me back to Philly so's I could plead guilty, an' I was standin' there in my big fur coat an' all an' everybody lookin' cause they never seen no colored woman in a limousine with no damn fur coat on her back before so the Judge takes one look at me an' says a year an' a day. An' I didn't tell no damn body I didn't know nothin' about any of that shit till I met you, Sonny. An how you cried so bad when I wouldn't have none of it, an' said nobody ever loved you enough to try a little bit of a hit or two with you an' I said I would but not heroin, an' you was so lonely an' scared an' said nobody who didn't try it couldn't know what it was like for you. An' so . . . I said to myself Sonny'll know there's one damn bitch in this world that loves him.

[MUSIC # 16: HUSH NOW]

(BILLIE starts singing "DON'T EXPLAIN.")

BILLIE. *(singing)*
HUSH NOW, DON'T EXPLAIN.
JUST SAY YOU'LL REMAIN.
I'M GLAD YOU'RE BACK. DON'T EXPLAIN.
SMILE. DON'T EXPLAIN.
WHAT IS THERE TO GAIN?
SKIP THAT LIPSTICK. DON'T EXPLAIN.

YOU KNOW THAT I LOVE YOU AND WHAT LOVE
    ENDURES.
ALL MY THOUGHTS ARE OF YOU
FOR I'M SO COMPLETELY . . . SO COMPLETE . . .

(SHE stops singing and hums along. SHE looks about, hunting the lyrics.)

BILLIE. (*singing*)
RIGHT OR WRONG DON'T MATTER. SMILE TO
  HEAR FOLKS . . . FOLKS . . . (*pause*)
OOO, WHAT A LITTLE MOONLIGHT CAN DO! (*The
  PIANO PLAYER switches to "WHAT A LITTLE
  MOONLIGHT CAN DO."*)
OOO, WHAT A LITTLE MOONLIGHT CAN DO TO YOU!
YOU'RE IN LOVE, YOUR HEART'S AFLUTTER
  'CAUSE ALL DAY LONG YOU CAN ONLY
  STUTTER . . .

BILLIE. You know what I want? I want me a beautiful home.
An' . . . an' some kids. An' . . . an' I want to cook. An'
somethin' else. I want a club. My own club. Very small. Very
cozy. Where I can sing to all my friends. That's all. What else is
there?

[MUSIC # 17: DEEP SONG]

(*BILLIE sings "DEEP SONG." The PIANO PLAYER follows
  her. Everything should appear normal until BILLIE sings the
  line, "Love lives in a barren land where there's no helping
  hand to understand."*)

BILLIE. (*singing*)
LONELY GRIEF IS HAUNTING ME
LIKE A LONELY SHADOW HAUNTING ME.
IT'S ALWAYS THERE JUST OUT OF SIGHT
LIKE A FRIGHTENING DREAM ON A LIGHTNING
  NIGHT.
LONELY WINDS CRY OUT MY NAME
SAD AS HAUNTED MUSIC IN THE RAIN.
IT'S GONNA BE BAD, THAT I KNOW.
BUT I HEAR IT CALL AND I'VE GOT TO GO.

WHERE CAN I BE HEADED FOR?
THE BLUES CRAWLED IN MY DOOR TO LICK MY
  HEART ONCE MORE.
LOVE LIVES IN A BARREN LAND WHERE THERE'S
  NO HELPING HAND TO UNDERSTAND.

(*After SHE has sung this line, SHE seems to continue the song, but no audible sound escapes her mouth. SHE mouths the words. All the way through the last half of the song — but her voice is not heard again. The PIANO PLAYER unaware as BILLIE herself to this phenomenon continues playing the song.*)

BILLIE. (*silently mouthing*)
WHY DOES IT BRING THIS ACHE TO ME?
WHY? IT DON'T MATTER WHY!
I ONLY KNOW MISERY HAS TO BE PART OF ME.
NEVER HOPE TO COUNT ON LOVE . . .
TO BE A PARTNER OF THAT HEAVEN UP ABOVE
NEVER HOPE TO UNDERSTAND
LOVE IS A BARREN, A LONELY LAND
A LONELY LAND.

(*Her voice is stilled but the PIANO PLAYER plays to end of song — oblivious to her silence.*)

CURTAIN.

END OF PLAY

SETTING

The set for LADY DAY AT EMERSON'S BAR & GRILL can be as simple as a bare platform with a piano, a piano stool, a microphone and a high stool or bar stool for Lady, or as elaborate a re-creation of a sleazy bar as the director wishes. The play has proven equally effective in each kind of production.

PROP LIST

piano and piano bench
a high stool or bar stool
a microphone
a water glass
gardenias
white fingerless three-quarter length gloves

"14"

Piano

microphone

Swinging
Door

Bar Counter

Smoke on the Mountain

BOOK BY   CONCEIVED BY

Connie Ray   Alan Bailey

MUSICAL ARRANGEMENTS BY

Mike Craver & Mark Hardwick

"Perfectly delightful"
The New Yorker

"A charming and funny celebration of America"
The New York Times

"Totally beguiling …Not to be missed"
New York Post

"A sophisticated audience went simply wild"
Philadelphia Daily News

"A rollicking blend of monologues and musical numbers"
Variety

The year is 1938. It's Saturday night in Mount Pleasant, North Carolina, (home of the Mount Pleasant Pickle Factory) and the Reverend Oglethorphe has invited the Sanders Family Singers to provide an up-liftin' evening of singin' and witnessin'. The audience is invited to pull up a pew and join the congregation for a rollicking good time. More than two dozen songs, many of them vintage pop hymns, and hilarious stories from the more or less devout Sanders family members provide a richly entertaining experience that is evocative of another era. 4 m., 3 f. (#21236)

MUSICALS WITH CHRISTMAS SPIRIT

SCROOGE!

BOOK, MUSIC AND LYRICS BY
Leslie Bricusse

"Wonderful theatre."
Yorkshire Evening Post

"Sensational.... It was terrific."
BBC Radio

"Just wait until you see *Scrooge!*"
Radio 3 – Australia

This is the wildly successful stage version of the classical movie musical based on *A Christmas Carol* which starred Albert Finney. Adapted by a renowned writer-composer-lyricist, it is an easy-to-produce show to delight audiences during the holiday season. CD available. (#21029)

Sanders Family Christmas

WRITTEN BY   CONCEIVED BY
Connie Ray   Alan Bailey

MUSICAL ARRANGEMENTS BY
John Foley & Gary Fagin

From the creators of the
"perfectly delightful,"[1] "totally beguiling,"[2]
"charming and funny"[3] musical comedy
SMOKE ON THE MOUNTAIN

It's December 24, 1941, and America is going to war. So is Dennis Sanders of the Sanders Family Singers. Join Pastor Mervin Oglethorpe and the memorable Sanders family as they evoke some down-home Christmas cheer with hilarious, touching stories and 25 bluegrass Christmas songs. Here is a richly entertaining musical that has audiences clapping, stomping and singing along with the *SMOKE ON THE MOUNTAIN* crowd. (#20948)

[[1]*The New Yorker,* [2]*The New York Times,* [3]*New York Post*]

POPULAR MUSICALS
from Samuel French

After the Ball

Avenue X

The Best Little
Whorehouse in
Texas

The Big Bang

Blood Brothers

Chess

Chicago

Clue:
The Musical

Das Barbecü

Eating Raoul

Do Patent
Leather Shoes
Really Reflect Up?

Doctor! Doctor!

Evelyn and the
Polka King

The Gig

Grand Hotel:
The Musical

Grease

The Green Heart

Gunmetal Blues

It Ain't Nothing
But the Blues

James A. Michener's
Sayonora

James Joyce's
The Dead

Kiss of the Spider
Woman

La Cage aux Folles

The Last Session

Leader of the Pack:
The Ellie Greenwich
Musical

Little Mary
Sunshine

Mack & Mabel

Me and My Girl

A New Brain

New York Rock

AVAILABLE FOR MANY SAMUEL FRENCH MUSICALS
Original Cast Recordings on CD
Demo Tapes
Promotional Posters